The Dreadful Truth

Confederation

Ted Staunton

**Illustrations by
Graham Pilsworth**

Formac Publishing Company Limited
Halifax, Nova Scotia

Formac Publishing Company Limited acknowledges the support of the Cultural Affairs Section, Nova Scotia Department of Tourism and Culture. We acknowledge the financial support of the Government of Canada through the Book Publishing Industry Development Program (BPIDP) for our publishing activities.

We acknowledge the support of the Canadian Council for the Arts for our publishing program.

National Library of Canada Cataloguing in Publication

Staunton, Ted, 1956-

      Confederation / by Ted Staunton ;

illustrated by Graham Pilsworth.

(The dreadful truth ; 2)

ISBN 0-88780-630-9

      1. Canada—History—Confederation, 1867—Juvenile literature.

2. Constitutional history—Canada—Juvenile literature. I. Pilsworth, Graham, 1944-

II. Title. III. Series: Dreadful truth ; 2.

FC474.S73 2004   j971.04'9   C2004-900553-7

This book is printed on acid-free paper that is 100% ancient-forest friendly (40% post-consumer recycled).

Formac Publishing Company Limited

5502 Atlantic Street

Halifax NS B3H 1G4

www.formac.ca

Printed and bound in Canada

Contents

The founding of Canada… Excuse me while I yawn.

We all know the boring stuff about Confederation: old guys with bad hair droning in a room.

Americans have action; we have conferences.

Okay, we did have action *once*, way back in the rebellions of 1837 in Upper and Lower Canada, when colonists said, "Enough top-down bossing around!" Luckily for them (but unluckily for action fans) the result was the Durham Report:

it created the Ontario-plus-Quebec colony of Canada and an elected, or responsible, government. What it really meant was thirty years of elected guys with bad hair, arguing in rooms.

Welcome to boredom.

That's where this book comes in. This is the good stuff — the sex, drugs, and polkas of Confederation. There was plenty going on that was — as they said of Lord Byron — mad, bad, and dangerous to know. Odd things, funny things, frightening and just plain weird things too. Stuff they don't always tell you. It's all here, in ten short chapters, with pictures. As the dads of confederation might have said, what a deal.

You and Then 1

History mystery

Ever get that feeling how totally weird it is to be you? If one thing had been different, you might be someone else — you, but not you.

That feeling is what history is about: asking why, what if, what was important? In other words, how the heck did we get here? It's tricky, because the past is us, but not *us*.

Sometimes things in the past look familiar to us now but meant something very different then. Sometimes things looked different but were really much the same as today. History takes getting used to for it all to make sense.

The basics were there in the 1860s: families and friends, brothers who bugged you and buddies who didn't. There was skating and swimming and stories and secrets.

There were the same places too, but no "country," just five zit-sized colonies: Newfoundland, Prince Edward Island, Nova Scotia, New Brunswick, and "Canada," i.e., Ontario plus Quebec (Didn't you read the Introduction?) And nothing west of the Great Lakes.

So far, so good. But, besides a population, a few other things were missing: telephones, libraries, hockey, movies, pop, cars, comics, CDs, lip gloss... In fact, forget electricity, tap water, and indoor toilets. There was money, but not much. Most people earned maybe a dollar a day.

Laissez les bons temps roulez

Let the good times roll. So what was there a lot of? How about SMELLS. Sweat, smoke, manure, open drains, bad meat, and poop in a pit would be old friends no matter where you lived. Oh, yum.

MUD. The good stuff: knee deep and climbing. Roads weren't paved, anywhere.

BROTHERS AND SISTERS. You had to grab fast at the dinner table; families were big. Babies and little kids tended to die, because medicine was either non-existent or booze in disguise (see DRINKING). With lots of kids, the odds were better that

some would survive to help Mom and Dad — as long as Dad didn't die in an accident or Mom giving birth to another brother or sister.

CONTESTS. Guys showed they were guys in contests. Lifting hay bales, *mano a mano* eating (dozens of raw eggs, or frozen ants off a maple stump), canoe racing, and wrestling were all big favorites. These were followed by major tummy trouble, sweat, and more SMELLS.

DRINKING and DRUNKS. Happy hour was all day. Beer was safer than town water. A nickel bought a quart of brew with a major kick. For the same price you could get a "grunt": all the whiskey you could guzzle without taking a breath.

Need a painkiller? Booze. Baby crying? Booze and water helps it sleep. Tired of shopping? A bucket and a dipper in the back of the store; free snorts for customers. Live in the country? Make your own.

Alcohol was the Great Escape everyone could afford. Or could they? A lot of wages glugged away on payday. This was money big families could have used. Over half the people in Toronto's jail were sobering up.

BEES. Not the buzzing kind. A bee was a get-together for fun and work at the same time. Country women might gather for sewing, whole families would slog through MUD for a barn raising. After, there might be CONTESTS, and maybe DRINKING, which might lead to...

DANCES. Just add a fiddler, footwork, and probably more DRINKING.

EXECUTIONS. A good public hanging beat a fleabag circus or travelling show any day. Best of all, it was free. You'd bring a picnic, drag along your BROTHERS AND SISTERS, avoid the MUD and DRUNKS and, well, hang out.

FUNNY MONEY. British, American, and colonial cash was floating around, and it was easy to counterfeit. Bartering was safer and kept money out of the hands of DRUNKS.

NEWSPAPERS. No TV or radio? Newspapers ruled. You didn't have to read to get your money's worth. Paper was heavy, made from rags, straw, and cotton instead of wood pulp. Newspapers made great insulation under blankets and coats, filled in cracks, doubled as wallpaper — and finally, ahem, bottomed out in the outhouse.

The worst for last

The thing there was most of, though, was WORK. Until you got rich — and not many did — you WORKED, no matter what your age. Forget sports, forget hobbies; even school was so far down the list that settlers without kids were known to burn down the schoolhouse so they didn't have to pay education taxes.

And we're talking *work* WORK. Kids drudging on the farm, sunup to sundown. Hauling coal in the mines seventy hours a week. Being paid piece-by-piece for making shoes, candy, clothes, or cigars. Learning a trade by apprenticing free for seven years. If all those BROTHERS AND SISTERS survived and your family got too big, they might stick you in an orphanage. The orphanage would, yup, hire you out to WORK.

So what's with this Confederation stuff?

Folks WORKING so hard didn't have time for fancy talk about constitutions or confederating the colonies. Only the boys at the top did. To them, squeezing five tiny zits into one medium-sized pimple was just the beginning.

Some of these guys had plans, big plans. Plans so big they seemed almost crazy. There were barely enough people in the five zits to make one decent colony, but these guys wanted to grab that empty West too. They wanted to hook up with microscopic settlements thousands of miles away on the Pacific coast, by building a railroad. In other words, they wanted one honking, coast-to-coast country.

Call it vision, call it passion, call it patriotism, call it being scared of gorillas (see Chapter Three), call it a naked lust for money, power, and a knighthood or four. Call it wanting a better life.

Well, *everyone* came here for a better life, and part of that better life, since there was now responsible government, was getting to choose on Election Day. The big boys needed everyone's help. They'd gotten themselves all tangled up in a DEADLOCK, and there was this gorilla (Chapter Three, again) on the loose.

Imagine your way back there for a minute. Take a stroll through the MUD to the outhouse with your NEWSPAPER and read all about it.

Words and (Mis)deeds 2

The hole truth

It's 1864 and you're in the outhouse. You're out of the MUD, settled on the old two-holer. It's warm enough to be comfy and cool enough to keep down the SMELL. Now, take a look at that paper. Whatcha got, the Toronto *Globe*? The Charlottetown *Examiner*? The *Nova Scotian*? There's over three hundred to choose from.

Check it out. Three cents a copy. Tons of fun. It's one sheet, folded to make four pages. Except for page two, it's ads: miracle medicines (booze, remember?), hair restoring, buggy whips, mind readers, moustache wax, and other assorted weirdness for sale.

Page two is "news." There being no reporters, news is whatever an editor wants it to be — gossip, juicy bits from other papers (murders and fires are good), a romance serial, and usually a whole lot of enjoyable yelling about politics, which is where DEADLOCK and gorillas come in.

In the ring

Politics is the professional wrestling of 1864, except it's for real and, since there's no pro sports, the only game in town. It has heroes, villains, and cheating galore, and sometimes actual *wrestling*. In 1865 one clown pulls another's nose right in the legislature.

The paper you're holding cheers for one side or the other, because one politician or another probably owns the paper. Anyone who disagrees with him is an idiot, and stupid too, and the paper says so. Oops. Sorry, it *yells* so, which makes it more fun.

D(r)eadlock!

In 1864, as you perch on the backyard throne, a lot of the Canadian yelling you are reading is about DEADLOCK. Not a reggae hairstyle, DEADLOCK is a kind of political constipation, which makes the outhouse a good place to chat about it.

The French and the English get to elect equal numbers of representatives, even though there are more English Canadians as Ontario grows. The English want more power to change things, but the French are afraid of being swamped. The equal-numbers rule makes it a standoff.

Old Tomorrow

Not everyone hates a DEADLOCK. Conservative Party leader
John A. Macdonald is making a stellar career of putting things
off. Called "Old Tomorrow," Johnny is way more interested in
running whatever there is today. He can get just enough
support in English Canada to let him make a power-sharing
deal with the French, led by George-Etienne Cartier. Macdonald
and Cartier win election after election by not changing anything
but their undies.

Mind you, if you can't change anything, there's not much you
can *do,* either. The whole thing is a house of cards: too much
yelling and someone gets mad and it all crashes down, which
means another election.

It's a guy thing

Which is where you come in. You're parked in the outhouse, but the papers want you up and at 'em. Where can a guy get free DRINKS, free speech, and free-for-all fighting? A political rally! It sure beats eating ants off a stump.

But what if you're not a guy? Women play politics behind the scenes. They help round up support by organizing meetings and parties to get votes for their candidates.

"I'd rather have one woman canvasser than a dozen men," said one smart politician. Sure, but women still don't get to vote for another fifty-three years.

Putting your mouth where the money is

And so, if you own a little property, and you're a guy, you get to vote. And why is having a vote so cool? Because if the big boys need your help, they're ready to help back. For "Election Day," read "Payday."

See, voting is "open": you say your name, then your choice; no secret ballots in 1864. A candidate's helper will happily buy your vote, for cash, right at the door of the polling station. Bribes are so usual politicians have a standing joke: *My supporters can't be bought like* yours; *mine cost more.*

Party on

Drama, deals, dollars, and — *voilà* — DEADLOCK again. And then… nothing. *Nothing?* Well, not really, it's just that the next part of the paper has been... uh, used. But wait, what does this scrap say? *Cure for baldness?* No, down there! Of course, that's what's missing: *The Gorilla from Another Planet!*

Hairy Terror 3

Yes, the Gorilla from Another Planet, lurching north from a galaxy far, far to the south. Politicians heard its fearsome snuffle even as they yelled, and little hairs prickled on the backs of their necks.

You might know the feeling. You settle in to watch TV only to hear the alien life form from the room next to yours thundering down the hall. Usually it ignores you, but this time it snarls and grabs at the remote as if it's a ripe banana. These days, the Gorilla is (politely) called an older sibling. Then, it was the U.S.A.

The U.S.A. was big and hairy, and burping ammo — mostly at itself. Americans were fighting a civil war in the 1860s, partly over slavery in the South. By 1865 the war was over. The winning Northern army had more men in it than were living in all the colonies. Snorting and glaring commenced.

Mom always liked you best

And why were they glaring and snorting, you ask? Remember, every Teen Alien Gorilla has a bratty younger sibling, and that was us. We were the ones who fiendishly bugged them as they picked their pelts; masters of backing off just before they went berserk. You may know how to do this yourself.

Day to day, there were endless annoying little things that we did to them and they did to us:

They offered big bonuses to British army veterans to sign up in the Northern army.

We let Americans who wanted to dodge the army draft come here. (We did it again during the Viet Nam war.)

They started kidnapping likely soldiers out of border towns. You'd go for a drink in a tavern, be drugged, and wake up in the Union army.

We (and the Brits) made a bundle trading with the South. Halifax happily built ships for both sides, helping make the war last longer.

The Brits got so riled at the Americans stopping British ships and arresting people, they sent ten thousand troops to Canada, just in case.

We let Southern spies stir things up. As, for example, in the…

Ripping raid on St. Alban's

Southern spies mostly hung out at the St. Lawrence Hotel in Montreal and drank mint juleps. But in 1864 a gang of them, posing as tourists on a fishing trip (*hmmm*), crossed the border and went angling in the bank in St. Alban's, Vermont. They nipped back to Canada with two hundred thousand dollars in their nets. The Yanks complained. We caught the raiders, then let them off and let them keep the money. Washington was so mad it decided to cancel a trade deal, made it harder to cross the border, and talked about putting a navy on the Great Lakes. Oops.

Apologize to your brother

Why did we do it? Partly, we were snobs. Politics in the U.S., where everyone voted and they even elected judges, was clearly *way* more corrupt than our own, ahem, manly and

honest system. Plus, we didn't allow slavery. We were the end point of the Underground Railroad, the network of people that helped slaves escape the South. Forget that when they got here, we rarely made them welcome.

(There were even separate schools to keep black children from mixing with white.) Then, there was all that money to be made trading with both sides in the war. Finally, we figured that if things got really bad, the Brits would come to the rescue. We were still *their* colonies, after all.

Growing pains

So what do you do about a Gorilla from Another Planet? The short-run solution: bonk it on the head with the popcorn bowl, then lock yourself in the bathroom. The long-run: Mom won't come to your rescue forever, so you'd better keep growing.

In fact, Big Mama Britain was not thrilled about having to send over an army. It was expensive. It would be even pricier to float a navy on the Great Lakes to match the U.S. Big Mama started hinting that her kids should be big enough to look after themselves.

Canadians were cheap, but not stupid. The political boys knew that if the colonies banded together in a country they'd be bigger and stronger. They could link up railroads, trade, share defence, and nab that West before the Yanks beat them to it. And if Canada split into *two* provinces again, French and English, and each province did its own thing, they could even solve the DEADLOCK problem. Even Old Tomorrow could see that. He wouldn't mind running a bigger place, either. But that would be tomorrow. Someone had to stop yelling long enough to break the DEADLOCK today.

Browned off

Everything about George Brown was big. He stood six-foot four, with a big temper, a big mouth, and a big newspaper, the Toronto *Globe*. He was a big shot in the little colony of Canada, head of the Grits, or Liberal party. Among other things, he hated Catholics, French-Canadians, Corruption, and Conservatives, particularly John A. Macdonald (Macdonald had accused him of making a shady deal, and Brown was mightily peeved) and George-Etienne Cartier.

The *Globe*, between hair tonic advertisements, wasted a lot of ink complaining about the DEADLOCK, but it didn't help. Brown could get himself elected, but not into power, thanks to Macdonald and Cartier's deals. This drove Brown crazy.

They loved him in the West (Ontario), and loathed him in the East (Quebec). Never Mr. Diplomacy, he called Cartier "that damnable little French-Canadian." What he called Macdonald we can't print. They didn't care, as long as they stayed in power.

It was a loud-mouthed, mat-slapping, DEADLOCKED tag-team yelling match, until Brown met … *her*.

The mom of Confederation

In 1862 Brown was depressed. He'd lost another election and business at the *Globe* wasn't so hot, either. He was middle-aged, bald on top, and minus a love life. Nowadays, guys deal with this by buying a sports car. Then, there weren't any, so he took a vacation instead, back to Scotland where he'd been born.

Not everyone would go to Scotland to cheer up, but it worked for Brown, especially after he met a girl named Anne Nelson. He swore off haggis and tried a comb-over. Sparks flew. Georgie and Anne got married and trotted back to Toronto, where they were met by five thousand cheering people at the train station, serenaded by a band, and led in a torchlight procession to their home.

It wasn't long before people noticed something. Not only had George changed his hair, marriage had mellowed him. Yes, love had turned the big lug into such a softy that early in 1864, he did the unthinkable: he declared in the legislature that he'd help *anyone* who wanted to end the standoff by creating a new country, a "Confederation" of the colonies. Each region could have its own government. The French could run the East, the English the West, the Maritimers the Maritimes. At the top you could put a central government to keep everything organized.

The DEADLOCK was broken. It was the legislature's turn to fall in love. Joy, as they say, was unconfined. A French-Canadian politician made a running leap into Brown's arms and gave him a surprise thank-you hug. Brown was suitably surprised. The person who really deserved the hug was Anne Nelson.

Just one problem

Confederation was not a new idea; co-operation was. And the timing was perfect: down in the Maritimes they were getting together in Charlottetown to talk about forming their own country. There was only one problem: Maritimers and Canadians didn't know each other, and the Maritimers weren't sure they wanted to. With all that Civil War boat-building business, the Maritimes were rolling in dough. They figured the Canadians for poor cousins with bad manners — always yelling at each other about language and religion. Nobody even had a map that showed all the colonies. They hemmed and hawed, then said politely, "We don't know if you should bother coming all this way. It's just a little get-together. You'd be bored."

"Not a problem," said the poor cousins, "what time is supper?" They were on their way.

Hitting the water

The conference in Charlottetown was supposed to start September 1, 1864. It was going to take the Canadians a while to get there. Roads were mud, covered with logs that jolted every bone in your body, not to mention breaking liquor bottles. Trains? Well, ten dollars got you from Toronto to Montreal, but summer wind blew cinders, sparks, and coal smoke through the windows. In winter snowstorms, you helped shovel. Worst, while the colonies all had railroads, they weren't linked together.

Movers and shakers don't like to be shaken as they move, so the future dads of Confederation decided to travel via luxury steamship, the *Queen Victoria*. They hopped aboard in late summer.

Who were those guys?

Apart from Brown, there were three dads-to-be to remember:
Macdonald, Cartier, and McGee.

John, eh?

Old Tomorrow was king of the deal. He only got excited about Confederation after Brown got the ball rolling and made a deal possible. His change of mind might also have had something to do with wanting a good party: he was a famously heavy drinker. (Once, blearily listening to a speech, he was sick all over his own shoes. When his turn came, he said, "Funny how listening to my opponent always does that to me." Which also goes to show how slick he could be.) Born poor in Scotland, Macdonald came to Kingston as a kid, managed to become a lawyer, and jumped into politics, where his charm and deal-making skill helped him ignore a spectacularly unhappy private life, and his hair and nose made him a cartoonist's dream.

Party, eh?

George-Etienne Cartier was a bouncy little party animal from Montreal who particularly liked leading after-dinner singsongs in French. This allowed him to sing all kinds of things to English listeners who didn't understand. A rebel against the government in 1837, Cartier was now making serious money as a lawyer for the Grand Trunk Railroad and running French Canadian politics. Under his shirt he wore a locket with a picture of Napoleon, and in his spare time he fooled around with his wife's cousin, who wore pants, smoked cigars, and read racy books.

Hey, McGee!

Wishing he was making serious money was D'Arcy McGee, a writer, of all things. Or, a writer of all things: poems, news stories, a novel, histories, speeches — anything that helped pay the rent. McGee was *another* charming boozer. (Macdonald once said to him, "McGee, the government doesn't have room for two drunks: you'll have to quit.") An Irish Catholic with a big family, McGee had come first to the U.S. as an Irish revolutionary, and then to Canada where he mellowed out.

And good looking, too

Bobbing gently down the St. Lawrence, the dads planned their sales pitch. McGee and Cartier were the good speechmakers, Macdonald was the fixer behind the scenes, and Brown was Mr. Honest.

They also spruced up. Looking at them now, this might be hard to believe. In pictures, these guys do not come across as the life of the party — or even alive.

First, blame the photographs. To take a picture back then you had to expose a chemical-coated glass or metal plate for up to a minute and a half. That meant you couldn't move — for a minute and a half. Try it. Hidden neck braces and head rests helped keep you still. If the dads look like they had steel rods up their rear ends, it's because they probably did.

Second, cut them some fashion slack. These guys were dialed for style. Clouds of unruly hair and extravagant side-whiskers (called muttonchops by the English, sideburns by the Americans, and ugly by women) showed you were a real Man. The long frock coat was picked up from England's Prince Albert. Underneath, a shirt with an upturned collar, a tie, and a vest to show off the chain for your pocket watch. Down below, narrow trousers, *unpressed* to look cool, and high boots (mud, remember?). And to show you were Serious: plain clothes and dark colours.

One more thing

The dads had an ace in the hole. Actually, a case in the hole: they brought along thirteen thousand dollars' worth of champagne, in case smooth talk and fashion sense weren't enough. Poor cousins, indeed.

Shall we Dance?

6

Looks can be deceiving

On the way to Charlottetown, the dads stopped off in Halifax to begin making nice. They were just in time for the Royal Halifax Yacht Club's annual Hodge-Podge and Chowder party. There, in their frock coats and watch chains, they got heavily into a game of (no kidding) leap-frog, which made them an instant hit. Clearly, being six-four gave Brown an advantage. Probably the champagne didn't hurt either.

Cirque de see-you-later

Flushed with froggy success, they floated on to Charlottetown, ready for a big howdy. Wrong-o. When they pulled in, the harbor was deserted. The first circus in twenty years had hit town just ahead of them, and no one was going to miss it.

The dads were all dressed up with no place to go. Finally a man from the government noticed them, borrowed a rowboat, and huffed out to officially welcome them. Landing, they had another treat: the hotels were full. All of which goes to show you: politicians are as loud as elephants, but not as popular.

Woodworking would work?

Our guys finally found places to stay. Macdonald, the comedian, checked in as a "cabinet maker." (*Government? Cabinet?* Get it?) The next morning twenty-three dads-to-be met in the legislature's Council Chamber, including a couple you should know.

Lenny Tilley, drug dealer

That's a grabber, huh? Okay, so Leonard Tilley owned a drugstore. The boss of New Brunswick was also a major Bible fan. This did not keep him from bribing voters when he had to. What he was against was drinking, although he didn't seem to mind the dads raising a glass or seven.

Chuck Tupper, wolf in sheep's clothing

The kingpin of Nova Scotia was Charles Tupper, a doctor. He was an arrogant, ambitious, humourless bully, and that's according to his friends. He was also quite the ladies man, known, ahem, as the Ram of Cumberland. His name, Tupper, was said to come from *tu perds*, French for "you lose," which pretty much sums up what a sweetie he was.

On with the show

The Council Chamber had gas-lamp chandeliers and a long wooden table. The boys sat around it in wooden armchairs, looked at each other, cleared their throats — and the Canadians swung into action. Macdonald winked and charmed. Brown oozed integrity. McGee and Cartier, the silver-tongued devils, talked.

Have we got a deal for you. Chance of a lifetime. As good as it gets. The big enchilada. Cards on the table. Trust us. Easy terms, no money down. Let's get together, but not too together — everyone likes a little space. Still, we're family, we'll care: remember birthdays, elect each other to look after things at the top. And we'll share: taxes, army, keep out the Yanks, join up the railroads, grab the West, share the WEALTH. And just for you, an added bonus: we've got some brand new parliament buildings up in Ottawa, haven't even taken them out of the box yet. Gothic revival, very classy, you'll love 'em.

They talked for eight days straight: rivers of words, followed by rivers of champagne. It worked. The Canadians stole the show. They were a bigger hit than the circus, which goes to show that champagne is even more popular than elephants among middle-aged guys with bad hair (except for Tilley). When the last cork had popped, the Maritimers swayed, burped gently, and slurred, *"Shounds good. Less talk shome more."*

"You bet," said the Canadians, *"Come to our house."*

With that, Tilley mixed everyone some bicarbonate of soda, Tupper went off to bully someone, and the Canadian dads climbed back aboard the *Queen Victoria*. They leap-frogged back across the Maritimes, then hurried home to tidy up. The cousins were coming in October.

Shall we Dance Again?

7

Company's coming

Back in 1859, Queen Victoria (the real one, not the boat) had royally squinted at a map and chosen a place called Ottawa as the capital for the colony of Canada, mainly because it was in the middle, between Toronto and Quebec City. She'd never been there, so how could she know the place was a dump? By 1864 Ottawa, except for the almost-finished parliament buildings, was still a dump, a tough Irish lumber town up to its eyeballs in mud. The dads, still worried about the "poor cousin" label, invited everyone to Quebec City instead. It was easier to sweep, plus it had that cozy French charm and a nice view. It rained for the entire seventeen days everyone was there.

Meanwhile, back at the fish farm

Down in the Maritimes, Tilley and Tupper and the gang realized this was getting serious. They were hot for Confederation, but then they were the ones who'd been drinking all that champagne (except for Tilley, of course). Other folks out their way weren't so sure. Solution: the Maritime dads invited some of the opposition along to Quebec. That way, they figured, if things went wrong they could all share the blame. If they did get a deal, there'd be enough champagne for everybody. Up the river they toddled, to what came to be known as "the great inter-colonial drunk."

How to friends people and influence win

The Quebec Conference was, shall we say, *festive*. The Maritimers were encouraged to bring families, appetites, and thirsts, and in no time at all they ran up a hotel tab of fifteen thousand dollars. (This, remember, when most folks earned maybe a dollar a day.)

Cartier sang and danced. McGee recited poetry. Macdonald backslapped. Brown beamed. And everyone drank. Parties lasted into the wee hours with "pushing, kicking, and tearing…of coat tails." True party animals, they left "the floor…covered with meat, drink, and broken bottles." A few nights into the parties, the Bishop of Quebec nixed "intimate" dancing — i.e., waltzing — just in case. We all know what intimate dancing leads to. That's right: playing cards.

Johnny the red-nosed reindeer

Sometimes, though, red noses lead the way. As the dads huddled in rainy, foggy Quebec, John A. became Rudolph. The champion boozer was the only dad who knew constitutional law. It was Old Tomorrow who got things done today, cutting deals, keeping everybody talking, fitting the details together, hammering it all out, and getting it written down so everyone could understand it. Cabinet-maker indeed.

What got written was a plan for how to run a new country. Cleverly, they called it the Quebec Resolutions. The dads were so pleased with themselves they kicked back and had a final, travelling party that took them all the way to Toronto, to finish up in style.

All they had to do now was convince the voters.

8

Way too much Fun

Tuponia?

For Confederation to happen, the dads needed a Yes vote from their colonial legislatures and an Okay from the British government. The British Okay depended on them getting their Yes votes at home, and so the fun began.

In Canada, this was no problem. Macdonald was so sure of it he took time off for a bender. And in fact, thanks to Brown, all but a few politicians were already on side. Thanks to Brown's paper, the *Globe*, most of the public was too. As the politicians voted yes, the *Globe* ran a Name the Country contest. Among the suggestions: Tuponia, Albinora, Laurentia, Transatlantica, Cabotia, and British Efisga (*E*nglish, *F*rench, *I*rish, *S*cots, *G*erman, *A*merican. Clever, no?).

O British Efisga...

Our home and native land...

One thing that was not suggested was a new flag. As loyal Britons, it was understood that we'd stick with the Union Jack. Canada didn't get a flag of its own until 1965, and then only after a huge flap, as it were.

Tu Perds

The bad news was that Tuponia was not an easy sell down in the Maritimes. As hangovers faded, sober second thoughts snuck in. Newfoundland and P.E.I. both backed out of the deal. Despite the hearty partying, they felt closer to the ocean and England than they did to champagne and Canada.

That left Nova Scotia and New Brunswick. The opposition had been for Confederation in Quebec. Now, seeing the public wasn't so sure, Tupper and Tilley's opponents saw a chance to get into power themselves by saying no to a deal. The dads stalled for time, putting off the votes until they could get popular support. The battle raged in the papers and outhouses of the colonies.

Howe now?

Leading the No forces in Nova Scotia was one man Tupper couldn't bully: Joe Howe. Howe was a — surprise, surprise — newspaper editor and politician, who'd been important since the 1820s. The man looked like a bulldog, and acted like one too. Way back in 1851 he'd predicted a coast-to-coast country. But he hadn't made it to Quebec and now, suddenly, the bulldog smelled a rat: Confederation would wreck Nova Scotia and make Canada rich.

He fired up his newspaper and yelled, "No." Nova Scotian support for Confederation sagged like yesterday's boxer shorts. Tupper sharpened his scalpels and kept on stalling, no matter how much Howe called for a vote. He was hoping that if Tilley got a Yes in New Brunswick first, it might help flip things back his way.

Tilley trips

The Lenster held out till spring 1865, then called an election over Confederation — and lost. Heavy hitters there didn't want to invest in a Canadian railroad, they wanted one to the U.S.A. Being practical, they did things the traditional New Brunswick way: they bought more votes than Tilley could, and Confederation was... sniff, sniff...

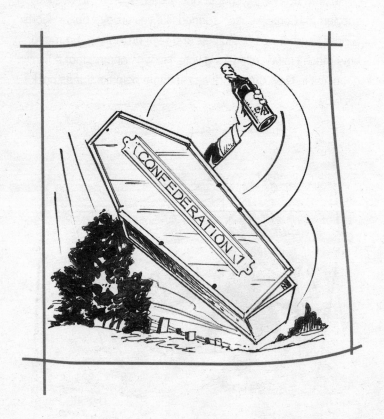

But wait...

You've heard the best offence is a good defence? Well, you should have. Tupper kept stalling, and — ta-da! — three things happened, all courtesy of the Gorilla from Another Planet from back in Chapter Three.

That loony-tunes bank job in St. Alban's had made the U.S. so mad it decided to cancel a trade deal with us. Suddenly a railroad south wasn't such a good bet.

Then, in 1865, the Americans' civil war ended. The North won. You could take your army rifle home with you for six dollars. This meant there was a whole bunch of unemployed guys with guns just south of the border. Hmm.

We got nervous. The Brits started hinting that maybe the Maritimes *should* hook up with Canada. Howe and friends didn't take the hint. The British started just plain saying it.

And finally, along came the Fenians, tripping north over their own shoelaces.

The Feeny yams?

Close. The Fenians were Irishmen living in the States who had apparently traded in their brains for sweet potatoes. They figured that if they invaded us, this would force the English out of Ireland. Their drinking song says it all:

> *Many a battle has been fought*
> *Along with the boys in blue*
> *So we will go and conquer Canada*
> *For we've nothing else to do.*

There's inspiration for you. By 1866, they still didn't have anything else to do, so a sad-sack bunch of them gathered at the New Brunswick border and made noises even worse than their singing. Then a smaller crew actually crossed the border near Fort Erie, Ontario. Out came the militia. There was a skirmish, and ten Canadians were killed.

The next day, with more militia on the way, the Fenians scuttled back across the border. The invasion was over. It was time to drink themselves cross-eyed.

Lenny leaps in

But nobody knew about the Fenian retreat yet. Everybody in New Brunswick was still so scared that there was another election. This time, things were different. People were seeing Fenians under the beds. The British were saying, "We *told* you to confederate." And, most important, with major cash from the Canadian Grand Trunk Railroad, Tilley out-bribed the opposition and bought the election back. With time out for a quick prayer, he passed a Yes vote. Before you could say forceps, Tupper yanked a Yes vote through on the rebound in Nova Scotia.

Steam shot out of Howe's ears. It didn't matter. It was also pouring from the funnel of the ship carrying the dads to England.

Pass the Peashooter 9

Dads will be boys

By now it was late 1866. Two years had gone by since those wild times in Quebec, and the dads and the British wanted to finish things up, whether everyone in the colonies liked it or not.

In London, England, they did some minor tweaking to the Quebec agreement, and gave it to the Brits. This left time for typical dad behaviour. On Derby Day, they got into the spirit of things at the racetrack, pelting each other with flour and firing peashooters into the crowd. Did these guys know a good time, or what?

Then Macdonald, working (and probably sipping) late in his hotel room, nodded off and knocked over a candle, setting fire to his bed and causing major damage, including some to himself.

Old Tomorrow, though, liked to say that if luck dumped a chamber pot on you, smile and say it was a summer shower. And in fact he cheered up considerably after running into Susan Bernard, a woman he'd met before in Canada. MacDonald, a widower whose first wife had been a drug-addicted invalid, caught fire faster than his hotel room. He promptly married her, proving he'd learned more than Confederation from George Brown.

Just a minute

But Joe Howe hadn't given up — yet. He panted over to England behind the dads to complain to the Brits. This Confederation stuff was all Tupper's doing, he said. Real Nova Scotians wanted to stick with Britain.

The Brits, however, didn't want to stick with them. Colonies were expensive. They told Howe to suck it up and go home. "Give it a chance," they said. "Ask Tilley for a headache pill. Don't call us; we'll call you."

Never follow a dog act

The British North America Act (B.N.A) sped through the British Parliament so fast it was embarrassing. The Brits had more important things on their minds: a bill about dog licences was really stirring things up.

Queen Victoria gave the B.N.A. Act the royal nod on March 29, 1867. As of July 1, there would be a new Dominion of Canada.

The big day

July 1, 1867. As the New Brunswick *Reporter* so stirringly put it, "From Halifax to Sarnia, we are one people." The sun shone. Bands played. Picnics were eaten. Horses were raced. Toasts were drunk. And drunk again. Cannon thundered on the Plains of Abraham.

Toronto kids got free Union Jacks. An ox was roasted at St. Lawrence Hall, and the meat given to the poor. George Brown wrote a gusher of an editorial that spilled off the front page of the *Globe*.

In Ottawa, soldiers cleverly fired a salute with the ramrods still in their rifle barrels, striking sparks on Sparks Street. In Halifax they struck sparks of a different kind. A crowd burned an effigy of Tupper, along with a live rat, thus becoming the first flaming separatists in Canadian history. The meat was not given to the poor. Elsewhere in the Maritimes, they settled for hanging black crepe in their windows. This was either a sign of mourning or an early start to Hallowe'en.

One whine, no women, and a pretty good song

The big day moved a Toronto schoolteacher named Alexander Muir to write a tune. He shelled out thirty dollars to print a thousand copies of the sheet music, titled *The Maple Leaf Forever,* and managed to earn back four dollars in total sales. There were no Canadian copyrights till 1868, so another publisher "pirated" the song without permission and made a small fortune. Welcome to the music business.

Father's day presents

The dads were in this for themselves, don't forget. Despite the horsing around, these guys were not best buds. As one writer put it, the dads didn't take each other by the hand, they took each other by the throat. Ambition and Jealousy were their middle names, and not everyone got what he wanted. Here's the rundown.

John A., I love you; I wish I could trust you

Old Tomorrow was the big winner, grabbing the spotlight, a knighthood (becoming Sir John), and getting himself elected Prime Minister in 1867. To make sure, he'd suggested an all-party government to start off the new country. Who was going to be more popular than he was?

In 1869, he found out his law business was a mess and he was bankrupt. In 1873, he lost the election over a railroad bribery scandal. Smiling under the chamberpot, he bounced back in 1878, charming, winking, drinking, and cutting deals. He was PM until he died in 1891. These days his nose and hair wave at us from the ten-dollar bill.

A different tune

Cartier, a long-time political partner, naturally got into Macdonald's cabinet, where he more or less ran things whenever the boss was too drunk. Still, he was royally peeved that he didn't get a knighthood. His after-dinner songs became untranslatable and he complained bitterly to everyone, including the new governor-general. He became Sir George. Later, he became half of the Macdonald-Cartier Freeway. Think of him as the passing lane; he was a fast guy.

Not to mention

Tilley and Tupper also supported Macdonald in the 1867 election, thus getting in the cabinet and becoming Sir Len and Sir Chuck. Tupper eventually became PM. The Ram of Cumberland, true to form, was sued by an American woman in 1891, who claimed he'd gotten her pregnant and then forced her to have an abortion. The meanest of the bunch, he was also the last to die, finally shuffling off in 1915.

Howe so?

British Bulldog Joe Howe snuffled home, licked his wounds, then started growling again. He and the other Nova Scotia anti-Confederationers got elected in 1867 and trucked off to Ottawa to stir things up. MacDonald deftly shut him down by giving Nova Scotia more money and offering Howe a seat in the cabinet. Howe instantly changed his mind about Confederation — again. For a bulldog, the guy sure could jump.

In fact the only better jumper was John A., who'd executed the deftest leap of all when he became pro-Confederation back in 1864.

The luck of the Irish

D'Arcy McGee, the poet of Confederation, paid a poet's price. As an Irish ex-revolutionary, McGee got no knighthood, but he was in the cabinet. Unlocking the door to his Ottawa boarding house one night in April 1868, he was murdered, shot at point-blank range by a Fenian, who believed McGee had betrayed his Irish roots. It is said that one hundred thousand people lined the streets of Montreal for his funeral.

Browned off

George Brown, the dad who got it all started, got burned. He declined Macdonald's all-party suggestion in the 1867 election, ran against him, and lost. There were no knighthoods for opponents out of political power. (No coincidence that all the other Sir dads were on Macdonald's side.) Brown quit politics and ran the *Globe*, after informing all the other dads that all the credit really belonged to him.

In 1880 a man fired by the *Globe* flipped out and pulled a gun on Brown in his office. Brown was shot in the leg and the wound became infected. He died, agonizingly, soon after.

Je me souviens

It's not only elephants that don't forget. Years later, Lady Macdonald and Mrs. Brown, both widows, were vacationing at the same spa in Scotland (where else?). When their carriages passed in the street, they made sure to look the other way.

In some ways, the same goes for us too. By 1869, Canada had bought the Northwest from the Hudson's Bay Company. By 1870, part of it was the province of Manitoba. In 1871, the promise of a railroad brought in British Columbia. P.E.I. signed on in 1873. Canada kept growing, with the last addition being Newfoundland, chugging into port in 1949.

But, like the widows, Canadians know how to hang on to a grudge. Our specialty is complaining that somehow, somewhere, someone else is doing better. On any given day you can hear Canadians in Alberta, Quebec, Newfoundland, and even Toronto grousing away like Joe Howe that Confederation is a rip-off and they ought to get out. Nova Scotians still think they were gulled by some fast-talking sharpies from Scarborough. Others note correctly that the rights of women and native peoples were not even considered by the dads. We still fret about the big bad U.S.A.

Unlike the widows, though, we manage to roll along in more or less the same direction. Long ago, D'Arcy McGee said that as long as we watched out for each other's rights and didn't give in to prejudice, we'd be safe. Here's hoping we can keep on doing just that.

OTHER BOOKS ON CONFEDERATION

Baldwin, Douglas. *Confederation and the West.* Calgary, Weigl
  Educational Publishers Limited, 2003.

Bliss, Michael. *Confederation: a New Nationality.* Toronto:
  Grolier Limited, 1981.

Careless, J.M.S. *Brown of the Globe* (vol. Two). Toronto:
  Macmillan of Canada, 1959–63.

Careless, J.M.S. *Canada: A Story of Challenge* (revised ed.).
  Toronto: Macmillan of Canada, 1974.

Conrad, Margaret, and Finkel, Alvin. *Canada: a National
  History.* Toronto: Pearson Education Canada Inc., 2003.

Ferguson, Will. *Bastards and Boneheads: Canada's Glorious
  Leaders, past and present.* Vancouver: Douglas and
  McIntyre, 1999.

Gillmor, Don, and Turgeon, Pierre. *Canada: A People's History.*
  Toronto: McClelland and Stewart Ltd., 2000.

Guillet, Edwin C. *The Pioneer Farmer and Backwoodsman* (2
  vol.). Toronto: University of Toronto Press, 1970.

Moore, Christopher. *1867: How the Fathers Made a Deal.*
  Toronto: McClelland and Stewart Ltd., 1997.

Stephenson, William. *Dawn of the Nation 1860/70.* Toronto:
  Natural Science of Canada Limited, 1977.

Waite, P.B. *John A. Macdonald.* Toronto: Fitzhenry and
  Whiteside Limited, 1976.

Waite, P.B. *The Life and Times of Confederation, 1864–1867.*
  Toronto: Robin Brass Studio, 2001.